I SPY
FUNNY TEETH

For Chalupa,
with great thanks to Dan
—J.M.

For Elizabeth Helt
—W.W.

Text copyright © 2003 by Jean Marzollo.
"Toy Chest," "Make Believe," "Odds & Ends," and "Cubbies" from *I Spy* © 1992 by Walter Wick; "Peanuts and Popcorn" and "The Laughing Clown" from *I Spy Fun House* © 1993 by Walter Wick; "A Whale of a Tale" and "The Hidden Clue" from *I Spy Mystery* © 1993 by Walter Wick; "Yikes" from *I Spy Fantasy* © 1994 by Walter Wick; "Mapping" from *I Spy School Days* © 1995 by Walter Wick.

Library of Congress Cataloging-in-Publication Data
Marzollo, Jean.
I spy funny teeth : riddles / by Jean Marzollo ; photographs by Walter Wick.
 p. cm.
Summary: Simple text challenges the reader to find objects hidden in the photographs.
 ISBN 0-439-52472-5
 1. Picture puzzles—Juvenile literature. [1. Picture puzzles.] I. Wick, Walter, ill.
II. Title.
GV1507.P47 M355 2003
793.73—dc21   2002015495

                 ISBN-13: 978-0-439-52472-8
                  ISBN-10: 0-439-52472-5
23 22 21   09 10

Printed in the U.S.A. 40 • This edition first printing, August 2008

I SPY
FUNNY TEETH

Riddles by Jean Marzollo
Photographs by Walter Wick

Cartwheel
·B·O·O·K·S·®

SCHOLASTIC INC.
New York Toronto London Auckland Sydney
Mexico City New Delhi Hong Kong Buenos Aires

I spy

a car,

a kazoo,

a horn,

a number game,

and a box of popcorn.

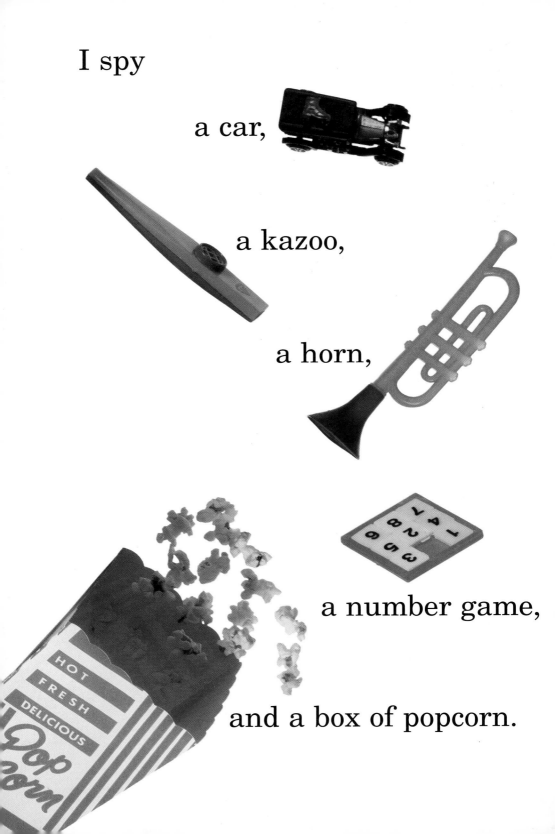

I spy

a tank,

two baseballs,

a clock,

a frog in a truck,

and a blue wooden block.

I spy

a guitar,

a fish,

a bow tie,

a face,

an axe,

and a butterfly.

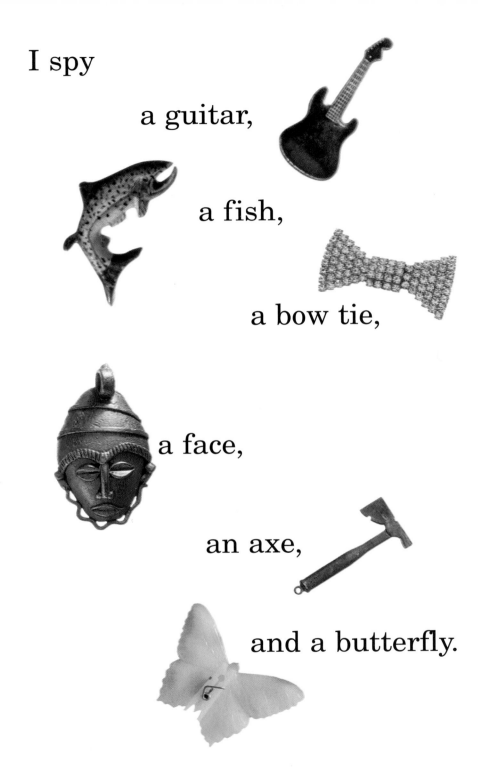

I spy

sunglasses,

a mask that's dark blue,

a clock,

a fan,

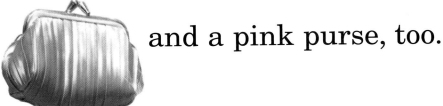
and a pink purse, too.

I spy

a green star,

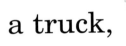 an apron that's white,

a truck,

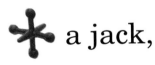 a jack,

and a red flashlight.

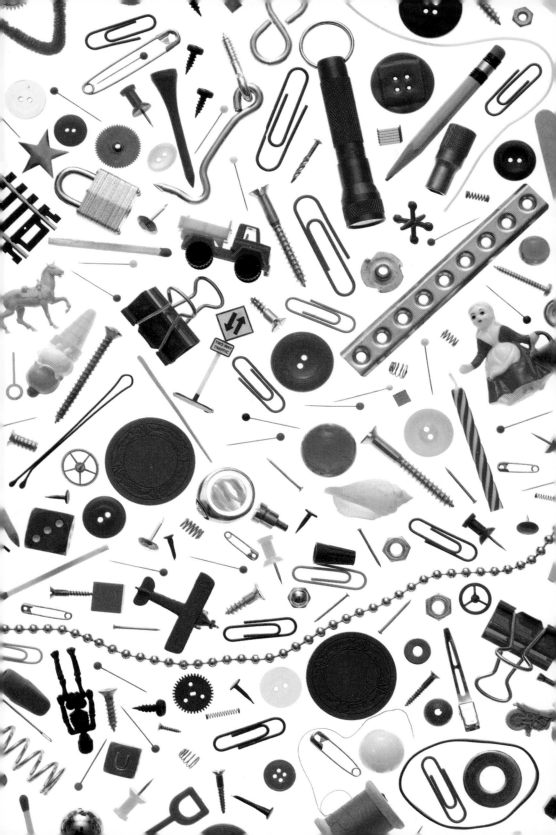

I spy

two gas pumps,

 a maze,

a bear,

four pink flowers,

and a clown's yellow hair.

I spy

a spoon,

 a basket of fruit,

two birds,

 an S,

and a cowboy boot.

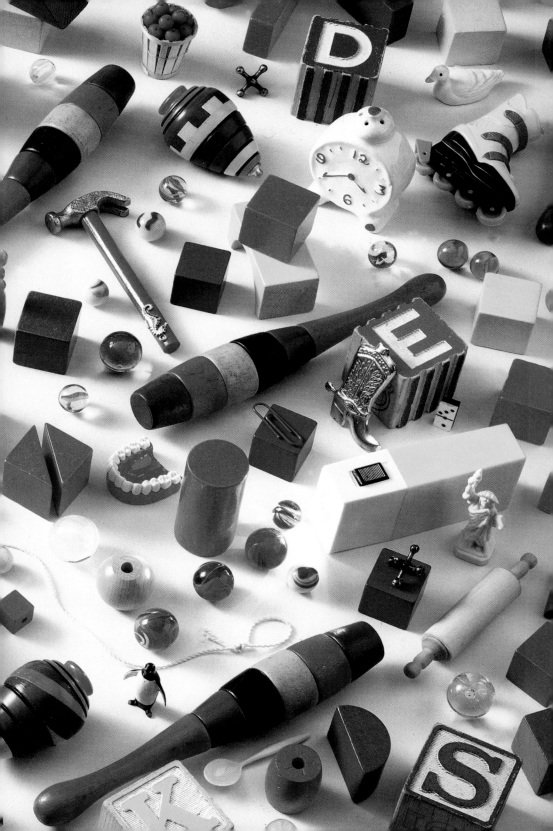

I spy

a giraffe,

 a marble,

 a king,

two googly eyes,

 and a blue-stone ring.

I spy

a domino,

 a big yellow Y,

funny white teeth,

 and a red bow tie.

I spy

five hats,

 three M's,

 an E,

a musical note,

and a zebra Z.

I spy two matching words.

red bow tie

fish

ball

red flashlight

I spy two matching words.

guitar

blue block

bus

blue mask

I spy two words that start with the letter B.

 butterfly

 face

 bear

horn

I spy three words that start with the letter P.

two gas pumps

 boot

pink purse

 truck

I spy two words that end with the letter S.

teeth

two googly eyes

car

two birds

I spy two words that end with the letters CK.

jack

game

zebra

truck

I spy two words that rhyme.

yellow Y

 bee on a car

clock

 green star

I spy two words that rhyme.

 basket of fruit

note

 cowboy boot

sunglasses

I SPY™

I SPY, You SPY, Let's all play I SPY!

SEARCH!

New I SPY video games include Ultimate I SPY for Wii™. A revolutionary way to play I SPY!

ESRB Rating: E for Everyone

PLAY!

New puzzles and games from  including I SPY Ready Set Silhouette and I SPY Flip 5!

WATCH!

Airs daily on

HBO Family®

For more I SPY Fun, log onto
www.scholastic.com/ISPY